Summit Series
'72

Also by Richard Brignall in the Lorimer Recordbooks series:

Summit Series '72

*Eight games that put Canada
on top of world hockey*

Richard Brignall

James Lorimer & Company Ltd., Publishers
Toronto

James Lorimer & Company Ltd., Publishers acknowledges the support of the Ontario
Arts Council. We acknowledge the financial support of the Government of Canada
through the Canada Book Fund for our publishing activities. We acknowledge the
support of the Canada Council for the Arts which last year invested $20.1 million
in writing and publishing throughout Canada. We acknowledge the Government
of Ontario through the Ontario Media Development Corporation's Ontario Book
Initiative.

Canadä

Cover design: Meredith Bangay

Library and Archives Canada Cataloguing in Publication

Brignall, Richard
    Summit series '72 : eight games that put Canada on top of world hockey /
Richard Brignall.

(Recordbooks)
Issued also in electronic format.
ISBN 978-1-55277-884-5 (bound).—ISBN 978-1-55277-883-8 (pbk.)

    1. Canada-U.S.S.R. Hockey Series, 1972—Juvenile literature. I. Title. II.
Series: Recordbooks

GV847.7.B75 2011   j796.962´66   C2011-903538-3

James Lorimer & Company Ltd., Publishers
317 Adelaide Street West,
Suite 1002
Toronto, ON, Canada
M5V 1P9
www.lorimer.ca

Distributed in the
United States by:
Orca Book Publishers
P.O. Box 468
Custer, WA USA
98240-0468

Printed and bound in Canada.
Manufactured by Webcom in Toronto, Ontario, Canada in August, 2011.
Job #379710

For Shelley

Contents

1 A Tale of Two Nations

Hockey has always been seen as a Canadian sport. Canada has shaped great players and strong teams. From the start, Canadians have known they were the top hockey country in the world. They could proudly say, "Hockey is our game."

But the United States and many European countries have played the game almost as long as Canada has. In 1908 a group of countries in Europe formed the International Ice Hockey Federation

(IIHF) to organize amateur hockey at an international level. It was the IIHF who introduced the first World Championship tournament in 1920.

The Canadian Amateur Hockey Association (CAHA) controlled amateur hockey in Canada. They decided who would represent the country at international tournaments. These picked teams became Team Canada.

Canada first started playing international hockey at the 1920 Olympic Games. The Winnipeg Falcons senior hockey club represented Canada in Antwerp. They easily defeated all competition. Team Canada returned home that year with their first gold medal in hockey.

But Canadians didn't take international tournaments seriously yet. The most important hockey games to them were played in the National Hockey League (NHL). Still, the CAHA always sent a team.

The 1928 Canadian Olympic hockey team was represented by the University of Toronto Grads. In the final game, they defeated Sweden to win the gold medal.

There wasn't much competition from the European clubs at that time. Almost any Canadian team that went won easily.

During this time, the Soviet Union was formed. The ruling Communist Party wanted it to be the most powerful country in the world. One way to do this was to show off their athletic greatness in sports. They wanted to break all the world records and win every championship.

Hockey was introduced to Russia in 1932. They slowly developed their hockey skills. They wanted to become good enough to compete against any country. Their plan was to win the World Championship and an Olympic

Birth of the Soviet Union

A single person called a czar once ruled Russia. The czar was the sole decider of what was right for the country. Many Russians lived in poverty as a result. In 1917, the people rose up and got rid of the ruling czar. Vladimir Lenin and Leon Trotsky led the revolution. They also helped introduce Communism to Russia. In 1922, the Soviet Union was formed. It was made up of Russia and 15 bordering states. After Lenin's death, Joseph Stalin took the Soviet Union to new heights. He wanted to take Communism worldwide. That led to the beginning of the Cold War between Communist-controlled "Eastern" countries and democratic "Western" countries.

gold medal. To meet that goal, they knew they had to be better than Canada.

A Russian hockey league was officially formed in 1946. In 1948 Europe's top team, Prague LTC, travelled to Moscow to play a team of Russia's best players.

Over 30,000 people attended each game in the series. Team Moscow defeated Prague 6–3 in their first match.

Nobody knew how well the Soviets would play against Prague. They surprised everybody and defeated the European champions in the three-game series.

Prague won the second game 5–3. The last game of three ended in a 2–2 tie. The Soviets declared themselves the winners, as they had outscored Prague 11–10.

"I do not have any doubt that the Soviet team will be able in short time to become the strongest team in the world," said a star player from Prague LTC.

In 1952 the Soviet Ice Hockey Federation became a member of the IIHF. By the spring of 1953 they were ready to enter the World Championship. But star forward Vsevolod Bobrov was hurt before the tournament, and the Soviets decided not to send a team. They were worried they would have a poor showing without Bobrov. Russian leaders did not like Soviet athletes or teams not finishing on top.

The Canadians were not aware of the

Soviet hockey program. They didn't know the Russians were planning to take over the international hockey scene. Canadians were still hardly interested in their own national team.

The Edmonton Mercurys were a good example of how Canadians felt about Team Canada. They had won the 1950 World Championship. They were also picked to represent Canada at the 1952 Olympics. Yet they got very little attention in their home country. There was only one reporter from Canada to cover the entire Winter Olympics. Any hockey scores that made it back to Canada sparked little excitement.

The Edmonton team's victory was quickly forgotten. Canada winning an international tournament was expected. Canadians were too used to winning.

That secure feeling would soon be gone. The Russians were ready to invade international hockey. The bitter fight to be the top hockey nation was about to begin.

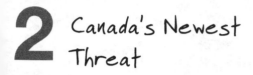

2 Canada's Newest Threat

Canada's greatest hockey rivalry started in 1954. That year, the World Championship was in Stockholm, Sweden. It was the first time the Soviet Union's national hockey team played in the World Championship tournament. Canada usually won the tournament with ease. They thought it would always be that way.

Canada couldn't send their best players to the World Championship. Their best players were professionals who played

In the 1950s, Russian players were the only ones to wear helmets.

in leagues like the NHL. Only amateurs could play at the World Championship or the Olympic Games. Unlike professionals, amateurs did not get paid to play hockey.

Every year, the CAHA had to find a team to go to Europe to compete. The best amateur teams played in Senior A hockey leagues. But the Senior A teams that were asked before the 1954 World Championship turned down the offer. The CAHA was forced to look at Senior B teams.

The East York Lyndhurst team was picked to represent Canada in 1954. They were runners-up in the Ontario Senior B Championship. The team was not the CAHA's first choice. But they were the best available team that wanted to go.

The Lyndhurst players were truck drivers and factory workers. They played hockey on weekends for fun. They might have been pretty good at it, but they were not quite good enough to play professionally. Now they wore sweaters with the word *Canada* across their chests. They represented their country against the world that winter. They didn't realize the weight of the responsibility that went with it.

When it was announced that Lyndhurst was going to represent Canada in Sweden, nobody wrote much about it. The sports reporters across Canada were too busy writing about the NHL.

At that time, any team that went from Canada won.

But as it got closer to the tournament, people began to worry about Lyndhurst. They were losing many league and exhibition games. Things didn't look good for them as Canada's national team.

To escape the pressure, Lyndhurst set out on a 13-game pre-tournament tour in Europe. The first exhibition game was in London, England. In front of 15,000 people, Team Canada lost 11–2. Back in Canada, the president of the CAHA scrambled to find an answer to the poorly picked team. He said better players would be sent to Europe to play for Team Canada in the World Championship games.

Lyndhurst was not as bad as people thought, though. They came back to win five straight games in Switzerland. In the end, they won 11 of 13 games against top European teams.

Still, European newspapers reported that Canada had no chance against the Russians. Lyndhurst was called one of the poorest Canadian teams ever sent to Europe.

The Soviets' 1954 debut at the World Championship was a success. They defeated the Czechs, the Federal Republic of Germany, Finland, Switzerland, and Norway. The only game they did not win was a 1–1 tie against a strong Swedish team.

Team Canada also looked good at

A Country by Many Names

The Soviet Union and its people were known by many names. The country's official name was The Union of Soviet Socialist Republics (USSR). The country was also known as Soviet Russia, the Iron Curtain, or simply Russia. Its people were called Soviets or Russians.

the tournament. They outscored their opponents 57–5 and won all seven of their games. They defeated Finland 20–1, Norway 8–0, and Sweden 8–0. Every team the Russians beat, the Canadians beat bigger. Canada only needed to tie the Russians to win the Championship.

The Canadians opened up with an attack-first offensive style against the Russians. It had been successful against other European teams. Dump-and-chase was the Canadian style of hockey. Players would quickly shoot the puck into the opponent's zone with three forwards chasing after it. On their way they crushed everyone and everything in sight. They fought hard for the puck. They used this strategy against the Soviets, but they couldn't score.

The Soviet team played the game differently than the other European teams. They didn't panic when facing the

Canadians. They had an offensive style that was hard to stop. Wave after wave of Russian attackers stormed the Canadian net. The Russians scored the first goal and just kept coming. After the first period, they held a 4–0 lead. Team Canada just couldn't find the trick to score on the Russians.

The Lyndhurst players felt the pressure of fighting for their country. They were nervous, and it showed in their performance. They were the top team in the tournament until that game. But it was that game that counted. It would be the one that people remembered.

The Soviets defeated Lyndhurst 7–2. The nearly 17,000 fans in the arena were in shock.

After the game, Soviet officials rushed onto the ice to congratulate their players. A red Soviet flag with the hammer and sickle on it was raised in celebration of their victory. The Canadian players stood in shame on their blue line. Some of them considered it the worst moment of their lives.

"Canadian youngsters are brought up to believe that we have the best hockey players in the world. Now they know only that the Russians beat us," said former NHLer Lionel Conacher. He called the Soviet victory a catastrophe for Canadian hockey.

There was an uproar across Canada the next day. They couldn't believe Canada had lost to the Russians. Reporters cared deeply about the tournament now that Team Canada had lost. They put down the Lyndhurst team. They put down the CAHA for sending them. They weren't used to a Canadian team losing. But they didn't have the whole story. They only knew that Russia had won. No Canadian reporters were there to describe the games.

Nobody reported how well Team Canada had played in the other seven games.

The Russians had become the top team in the world. Canada now had to fight to regain that position.

3 Penticton Versus the World

Canada's World Championship loss to the Russians succeeded in one important way. International hockey once again had the attention of Canadian fans. They wanted Canada to be number one again. They thought no other country could be better at hockey. They wanted only the best to represent Canada.

But the best players — the professionals — could not play international hockey. Canada had to send the best of the rest.

The CAHA couldn't decide whether to send the Senior A champions of Canada or to pick an All-Star team.

In the 1954 Senior A final, the Sudbury Wolves faced the Penticton Vees. Sudbury badly wanted to be the team that regained Canada's top spot at the tournament. But the Vees turned out to be the better team. They won the national championship. Later that spring, the CAHA announced that the Vees would represent Canada in the 1955 World Championships.

Penticton was a small town of 12,000 people in British Columbia. The backbone of the team was the Warwick brothers: Dick, Grant, and Bill. They were all tough, talented players dedicated to winning at any cost.

People in eastern Canada were not happy with the CAHA's choice. They didn't know anything about the Vees. People in the east hardly even knew where Penticton was. And they didn't want Canada to lose again.

It seemed like the only fans who believed in the Vees were the people in Penticton. For a while it seemed like it was the small town against the world.

The eastern Canadian newspapers said the team couldn't be good enough to win. "We listened to the uproar from the east all that winter," said Vees goalie Ivan McLelland. "Every game we played, we were being measured."

One sports reporter asked a Vees player, "What are you doing going over to Europe with this team from the West? You know you're not going to win nothing."

The World Championship tournament that year was held in West Germany. Not one Canadian reporter was there when Canada lost to the Russians in 1954. But it was a game that changed sports history. The scene was different in 1955. The best

The Penticton Vees stormed through Europe to win the World Championship. Here they are celebrating at a monument in Western Germany.

sportswriters in Canada went to cover it. They didn't want to miss the rematch.

When the Vees arrived in Europe, they played a few exhibition games. One game in Prague, Czechoslovakia, had been sold out for weeks. But the Canadians had been travelling for a week, and it showed. The Czechs were in great shape and the game ended in a 3–3 tie.

The next day, Canadian journalists wrote that the Vees needed help. The CAHA wanted to bring in some other players, but Vees Coach Grant Warwick said no.

To start the World Championship tournament, Canada defeated the United States team 12–1. Next came a 5–3 victory over the Czechs. It was during this game that the Canadians learned about European referees. On the ice, the Vees hit anything that moved. But what was considered regular play in Canada landed the Vees in the penalty box in Europe. The rough play turned the European crowd against the Canadians. But the Vees didn't care if the Europeans disliked it.

"Penticton played slam-bang, hard-skating, hard-hitting hockey and they had come a long way from BC to demonstrate that the Canadian style was best," wrote sports reporter Jim Coleman.

Over the course of the tournament the Vees also beat Poland, Finland, and Switzerland by scores of 8–0, 12–0, and 11–1. In their second-last game they defeated Sweden 3–0. That set up a final, winner-takes-all matchup against the Russians. Both countries were unbeaten.

It was going to be a tough game for the Canadians. Reporters from twenty countries were in the press box. Radio broadcasts would be in English, French, German, Czech, Russian, Dutch, Swiss, Polish, and Italian. Films were being shot for showings around the world. It was thought that hundreds of millions of people would hear or see the game.

People back in Canada were ready for this one. They listened to the coast-to-coast broadcast on CBC Radio. Canadian hockey fans wanted revenge.

It was up to the Vees to restore Canada's national pride.

For the final game, more than 10,000 hockey fans crammed into the arena. It had been designed to hold only 8,000. The 2,000 extra people included Canadian Armed Forces servicemen and women who were stationed on a military base in West Germany. The Canadian fans made ear-splitting noise from the opening faceoff to the final whistle. The Penticton players felt like they were playing in front of a hometown crowd.

Coach Warwick knew the pressure his team faced. Half joking, he told his team, "If you lose, you can't go home. You might as well go to China."

The Soviets had some truly great hockey players. But they were not ready for the tough checking they got from the Vees. Penticton's game plan was designed to control the Russian stars. They planned to check Vsevolod Bobrov closely. A scouting report showed he liked to hang around the red line, where teammates could easily pass to him.

The first time Bobrov took a pass and floated over the Canadian blue line, Hal Tarala was waiting for him. He delivered a shattering bodycheck to the Soviet captain. Bobrov was knocked high in the air. He twisted and landed headfirst on the ice. Bobrov was out of the game.

For the first period, it was the hockey game that people expected. It was a meeting of near-equals. Both teams skated with blinding speed. They moved the puck around with accurate passing.

Canada struck first when forward Jim Middleton got the puck against the boards in the Russian zone. He snapped a pass to Jim Fairburn. Fairburn then fed it to Mike Shabaga. Shabaga was alone in front of the net. He deked Russian goalie Nikolai

Puchkov out of position. For a split second it looked like Shabaga had lost the puck, but he quickly recovered it and scored.

A deafening roar came from the Canadians in the stands. Many yelled out "Go Vees Go!"

The Russians fought back hard. Five Soviet players kept the puck in the Penticton end. The puck buzzed around the Canadian goal. A couple of times it looked like they had scored, but the Canadian goaltender was always there to make the save. At the end of the first period, Canada was ahead 1–0.

Early in the second period, Vees forward Bill Warwick scored a goal. Mike Shabaga then scored his second to make the score 3–0 for Canada.

During the power play at the start of the third period, Bill Warwick was able to score the Vees' fourth goal. Two minutes later, George McAvoy drifted in a hot shot from the blue line that beat Nikolai Puchkov cleanly. Canada had a 5–0 lead.

Canada played two men short in the last 30 seconds of the game. The Russians still couldn't score. A last-second save by Canadian goalie Ivan McLelland saved his shutout, and Penticton won 5–0. They were awarded the World Championship trophy.

The Warwick brothers, Bill, Dick, and Grant, were the heart and soul of the Vees. Here they are celebrating with the championship trophy.

"We are very sure the better team won," commented one Russian sports official. "But we have learned some lessons. We will be back to show what we have learned."

The Vees were heroes back in Canada. At the centre of the celebration was Grant Warwick. He proclaimed over the radio, "God bless Canada! We brought the cup back home where it belongs and we'll keep it there!"

Penticton's Little Secret

Grant Warwick was right when he said the World Championship trophy would not leave Canada. His brother, Bill, had a copy made of that trophy. Before the 1956 World Championship tournament, he returned the copy to the IIHF. He kept the original on display in his restaurant.

4 Trying to Compete

The Vees' success led some fans to believe that the Soviets' victory the year before might have been a fluke. That theory was tested at the 1956 Olympics in Cortina, Italy. It was the first time the Soviet Union competed at the Olympics. Team Canada's players were from the 1955 Senior A champions, the Kitchener-Waterloo Dutchmen. They thought they were ready to defend Canada's national pride.

The Dutchmen were up against almost the same Russian team that played at the last two World Championships. But the Russians had learned from playing Lyndhurst and the Vees. Since their roster changed every year, Canada's teams couldn't take what they'd learned against Russia into the next year. Team Canada was always at a disadvantage.

The Soviets swept through the Olympic tournament. They won every game, including a 2–0 victory over Canada. The Soviet Union was awarded the gold medal. Team Canada placed third and won the bronze.

The international competition got tougher and tougher. Every year the World Championship ended with a battle between Canada and the Russian club. Sometimes Canada would win — but not always. That wasn't good enough for Canadian hockey officials. A gold medal and a perfect record were expected.

The Russians accepted their losses. They used them as lessons to make themselves better. That made them a dangerous threat to Canada's hockey supremacy.

Team Canada won the silver medal at the 1960 Olympics. Most countries would be happy with silver, but not

The 1961 Trail Smoke Eaters were the last Canadian amateur team to win the World Championship. They couldn't repeat that success when they represented Canada again in 1963.

Canada. Canadian hockey officials looked for answers to a simple question: "How can Canada be on top again?"

Canada had to change the way it played international hockey. The idea was brought forward to form a Canadian National Team. The CAHA knew that regular senior teams were no longer good enough to represent Canada internationally.

Father David Bauer saw his chance to submit an idea he had. The junior coach approached the CAHA and suggested they form a permanent National Team. It would be based at the University of British Columbia. He said lots of junior players were in favour of any plan that would let them go to school and play hockey at the same time.

The CAHA liked his plan. The 1964 Olympics were approaching, and they needed an amateur team to represent Canada. Father Bauer's idea was accepted.

He needed to attract some of the

country's best junior hockey players to the team. But the players he wanted were often the same ones professional clubs wanted. The pros offered money. Father Bauer offered a place to stay, schooling, international travel, and the national program. His deal won out with many players.

In the summer of 1963, 30 young players reported to the team's first training camp. At the end of the second week, Father Bauer picked 22 players who would be the first Canadian National Team.

The 1964 Olympics were held in Innsbruck, Austria. Canada's National Team was undefeated going into their final two games. Their first real tests were against Czechoslovakia and Russia. Team Canada lost both games.

Russia finished the tournament with a 7–0 record. Canada, Czechoslovakia, and Sweden all had 5–2 records. When

Canadian newspapers did not hold back their criticism of Team Canada. During the 1960s, they saw the team as a poor representative of Canadian hockey.

the medals were handed out, Russia received gold, Sweden received silver, and the Czechs received bronze. Team Canada placed fourth. But the CAHA was pleased, and decided to continue the National program.

In 1965 the city of Winnipeg became the new home for the National Team. That year, Team Canada had its worst World Championship showing. They finished fourth with a 4–3 record. In 1966 they improved only slightly to third place. The Canadian team still couldn't get past Russia or the Czechs.

Nobody in Canada understood what the National players were up against. They were stuck in the old days, when any Canadian team could win without much effort.

"All they know is that we lost and they don't care how," said a National Team official.

"The Russian equipment was quite poor and yet they could do better things than we could. They never had the skates we had. They never had good hockey sticks," said one National Team player. "When we did begin to believe how good they were, it was even more frustrating trying to tell Canada that. They used to laugh. They'd say 'Oh, we just have to take some pros over, knock them off their feet.'"

The gap between Russia and Canada was widening, largely due to the coaching of the Russian squad. The man behind the Soviet team was Anatoli Tarasov. He was called the father of Russian hockey. He developed his own system of play based on skating skills, speed, and precise passing. Tarasov transformed Russian hockey forever.

Tarasov wasn't influenced by Canadian hockey. He knew to succeed against

Cold War

At the end of the Second World War, a Cold War began between the Soviet Union and the United States. In a cold war, the two sides never meet in direct battle. Instead, they compete on every other level. The Soviets and Americans struggled to have the biggest army and the most nuclear bombs. They raced each other to the moon. They fought for scientific and technical supremacy. They also fought to see who had the best athletes. "Us vs. Them" became a rallying cry for both sides. Canada was caught in the middle.

Canada, the Soviets could not copy the Canadians. Soviet hockey players had to create their own school of hockey.

"I am sure that if we tried to copy the Canadians we would be doomed to play second fiddle forever," said Tarasov.

Tarasov believed hockey players should be all-around athletes with speed and strength. The Soviets trained harder than any other team. They repeated basic plays and tactics many times until they perfected them. They wanted to be able to dominate every opponent. Perfection was their goal.

Tarasov believed teamwork was another key to success. There were no stars on the National lineup. "One player, no matter how good he is, cannot outplay a whole team," said Tarasov.

"Players, as they advance, pass the puck up the ice in an effort to outplay the opposing team by teamwork," said Tarasov. "Soviet players pass much more than the Canadians. The greater number of passes increases the effect of an offensive attack."

Tarasov called his approach the "creative" or "attacking" style of hockey. It was built on speed, mobility, teamwork, and passing. He called the Canadian style "power hockey" because it was built on bodychecking and intimidation.

The Soviet players took over international hockey with their new system. Not even Canada had a team strong enough to defend against them. There were only two or three Canadian National players who could even have made it onto the Russian team. People asked, "So how can Canada win against them?"

5 Last Straw

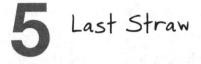

Canadians couldn't accept Team Canada's failures on the international hockey scene. For many years the government didn't get involved with sport. But it looked bad for the country if they kept losing. The Canadian government stepped in to help create Hockey Canada.

Hockey Canada was formed with two goals. First, they wanted to make Canadian hockey well respected again on the international scene. Second, they wanted to help the growth of amateur hockey in Canada.

The 1969 World Championship was held in Stockholm, Sweden. It was Hockey Canada's first test as head of the National Team. Canada only won four of ten games. Russia won the gold.

Father Bauer's dream ended with that tournament. Hockey Canada started to talk with the IIHF about Team Canada using professional players. Canada wanted the World Championship to become an open competition for pros and amateurs. Hockey Canada thought that was the only way they could compete internationally.

At first the Soviets agreed to pro players on the Canadian team. They wanted to be tested. So the IIHF agreed to let Team Canada use professionals.

In the fall of 1969, a Team Canada stocked with professional players played in an international tournament. They played a little too well. The Soviets had a change of heart about playing Canadian pros.

A group of Soviet hockey officials met to talk about this change in hockey. They didn't want to disturb the fake amateurism they played under. The Russians and other European teams made no attempt to separate players who made a career of hockey from those who did not. These players were really professionals, but they were still called amateurs. In Canada, about 700 openly professional players had to be automatically excluded when the National Team was put together. That put Canada at a great disadvantage.

If the Europeans played a professional Canadian team, they would lose their amateur status. They would be banned from the Olympics. So the European countries changed their votes at the next IIHF meeting. They banned Canadian professionals again. Countries like Russia, Sweden, and

Czechoslovakia voted against Canada.

Canada was preparing to host the 1970 World Championship. But Hockey Canada stood its ground. They still wanted to use pro players. When some European teams refused to play, the tournament was moved to Sweden.

In protest, Hockey Canada withdrew from all international hockey competition. They didn't send a team to the World Championship. They didn't send a team to the 1972 Olympics. Hockey Canada put a

The Eastern Bloc

The Soviet Union wasn't the only Communist country in Europe. The Soviets influenced many other Eastern European countries. Other Communist countries included Bulgaria, Czechoslovakia, East Germany, Poland, Hungary, Romania, and Albania. Communist countries around the world included Cuba, China, and North Korea.

total ban on sending teams of any age group to Europe. This put pressure on the European hockey clubs. They counted on the money made from touring Canadian clubs. Canada thought the Europeans would change their minds about professionals. But the Europeans also stood their ground.

Many Russian hockey officials were convinced that they had outgrown international amateur competition. They thought Russian players would stop improving if they couldn't play against the best Canadian pros. But they also felt that playing against pros was against Olympic rules. Like Canada, Russia put much value in an Olympic gold medal.

Russia won the gold medal at the 1972 Olympics in Sapporo, Japan. Their hockey officials almost immediately sent word to Canada that they wanted to talk about the future. They wanted to play Canada at hockey again. Canada could use anybody

Team Canada didn't get to play at the 1970 World Championship. It would be many years before another amateur team represented Canada.

they wanted. The Russians would play NHL teams, All-Star teams, or whomever Hockey Canada could come up with.

Canada finally got their wish. It was Canada's best against Russia's best. Many people argued for almost 20 years that a team of top Canadian professionals could easily defeat the Russians. Team Canada was in for the shock of their lives.

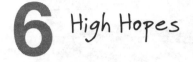

6 High Hopes

Canada and the Soviet Union were very different countries in 1972. Canada was a free, democratic society. The Soviet Union was a closed, Communist-controlled society.

Canadians were scared of the Soviet Union. For decades, children were taught to fear communism. They were used to seeing images of tanks and missiles being paraded around Moscow's streets. Democratic countries didn't always

Communist Control

Communism is based on Karl Marx's idea that in a perfect world everyone would have food and shelter. He thought there should not be any divisions in society. No one would be rich or poor. In this society, the government would control everything. Marx inspired the formation of the Communist party in the Soviet Union. At the height of its power, the Soviet Union became a closed society. It was a mystery to those outside its borders, including Canada.

agree with Communist countries. A war between the two sides was a Canadian's worst nightmare.

It was hard to believe that both countries loved hockey. But hockey provided a common ground for them to begin to know each other better.

Hockey Canada arranged an eight-game series between the two countries. Four games would be played in Canada and four in the Soviet Union. They were scheduled for September 1972. They called it the Summit Series.

Harry Sinden was named Team Canada's head coach. He was a former NHL coach with an eye for talent. Former hockey player John Ferguson was named his assistant. Team Canada would include the best players in the NHL at that time.

Team Canada's training camp opened at the beginning of August. Some players thought all they had to do was show up and defeat the Russians. They didn't train hard. They thought just because they were NHL players they could not be defeated.

"I look around and see the quality of the players here and wonder who could beat us," said Team Canada forward Bobby Clarke.

Before the series, Team Canada sent two scouts to report on the Russian team. They brought back good news. They said only one player on the Russian team could have made the NHL. They thought Vladislav Tretiak wasn't much of a goalie, even against weak Soviet shooting. They reported the Russians didn't know how to do a slapshot. Their defence was slow. Their passing was slower, and could easily be broken up by any NHL player. They didn't think the Canadians should worry about the Russians.

Every journalist across the country thought Team Canada would sweep the eight-game series. Only one reporter thought differently. John Robertson of the *Montreal Star* thought Russia would win six of eight games. His view was not very popular.

Sinden tried to warn his team about the Russians. He had previous experience against them when he was a player. But no one believed him.

"We did not have enough fear of our

opponents," said Team Canada goalie Ken Dryden. "We didn't respect our opponents. We didn't have a sense that we could lose."

Many of the Soviets were stepping onto Western soil for the first time in their lives. They were there to represent the entire Soviet Union. The pressure to succeed was felt by each player. They were uncertain of what to expect.

"I must say that we were afraid of them," said Boris Mikhailov. "We were afraid because, to us, the NHL team was something like a myth. We were afraid to lose big."

Sinden told his players to watch the Soviets' practice. When they got there, the first thing they noticed was the Soviets' poor equipment. That surprised the players. It only fuelled their belief that their opponents would be easily outclassed at every level.

"Judging by the gestures and behaviour of the Canadian players, there was a kind of arrogant attitude toward our team," said Russian player Alexander Yakushev.

At the Russian practice, there was no dazzling display of passing. There was no power shooting or flashy goaltending. The Soviets practised at a slow, low-key,

The 1972 Russian National hockey team was not seen as a threat to Team Canada. But their lineup was filled with the world's best players. They would give Team Canada a real fight.

even clumsy pace. Watching from the stands, the Canadian players grinned and smirked. They only saw soft shooting and stumbling defence. The Soviets didn't show everything that they really had while practising. Their display seemed to confirm the opinions of the Canadian scouts.

"I remember sitting and watching the Russians practice, and it looked like it was going to be a blowout," said backup goalie Eddie Johnston. "They screwed around, nothing went right, and they just looked awful. You couldn't help but wonder about the team."

"We watched their whole practice," said Vladislav Tretiak, whose Russian teammates studied the Canadians to find their strengths and weaknesses. "But they barely took five minutes to look at us. Our impression was they felt they could easily finish us off."

The Soviets attended every Team Canada practice. They watched films of past Stanley Cup games. They wanted to see how Canadian NHL players played. By the start of the Summit Series, they knew everything about Team Canada. And they had developed a plan to defeat the Canadians.

The Russians had won World Championships and Olympic gold, but they had never played NHL pros. They called it a test of their National program. Both countries' reputations were at stake.

7 Canada's Big Surprise

Team Canada had size. They had speed. They thought they had the talent to win.

"No one in North America took us seriously," said Russian goalie Vladislav Tretiak. "There was probably not one individual in all of Canada who would have had any doubt of a Canadian victory. And those views were not held only in Canada, as almost all Soviet fans favoured the Canadians."

The Montreal Forum was the venue

for the first game on September 2, 1972. A capacity crowd of 18,818 filled the stands. The arena was decorated in Team Canada's colours of red and white.

The Soviet team skated out onto the ice wearing simple red and white jerseys. Team Canada made its appearance in bright red uniforms. A large white maple leaf was printed on the jerseys and it seemed to wrap around their bodies.

"When we were introduced, our names were met with silence," said Tretiak. They were all unknown to the Montreal crowd. "When the announcer started to introduce the names of Canadian players, the crowd began roaring with such enthusiasm that my knees started to tremble. I actually felt fear."

It looked like the Soviets were right to fear Team Canada. They scored just 30 seconds into the game. Team Canada's top line of Phil Esposito, Frank Mahovlich, and

Yvan Cournoyer skated into the Soviet zone. They swarmed the Russian net. Mahovlich flicked a quick backhander that was kicked out by Tretiak. But Esposito was ready on the other side of the crease. He swung his stick at the rebounded puck and put it in the Soviet net.

It was just as the experts predicted. Everyone in the rink and across the country expected Team Canada to get goal after goal.

The Leader

Phil Esposito rewrote the NHL record book during his 18-year career with Chicago, Boston, and New York. He was the first player to surpass 100 points in a season. He once scored a league record 76 goals in 78 games. He won two Stanley Cups with the Boston Bruins. The two-time league MVP, five-time Art Ross trophy winner was inducted into the Hockey Hall of Fame in 1984.

The Canadians continued with their offensive pressure. Right off a faceoff in the Soviet end, Bobby Clarke passed the puck to linemate Ron Ellis. Ellis slapped it back to Paul Henderson, who stood at the top of the faceoff circle. Henderson one-timed the puck low and hard past Tretiak's outstretched pad and into the right-hand corner of the net.

"We all knew what the scouting report had said," said coach Harry Sinden, "and for the first couple of minutes that's how it looked. They looked like an average team with poor goaltending."

But even before Henderson's goal, people noticed how the Russians tore up and down the ice, making beautiful passing plays. They outskated Team Canada to loose pucks. They did everything but put the puck in Team Canada's net.

"It was right there that I knew the Russians were everything I didn't want them to be," said Sinden. "I just couldn't believe I was seeing the Russians go around and through us so easily."

Midway through the opening period, the Soviets began to relax. They found their legs and began playing great hockey.

"When we got up a couple of goals we were all saying, 'Here we go,'" said Peter Mahovlich. "Then all of a sudden it was, 'There they go.'"

At 11:40 into the first period, Yevgeny Zimin took a pass from Alexander Yakushev, and got past Team Canada goalie Ken Dryden. The Forum went silent. Few people believed the Soviets could ever get a puck past Dryden.

Before the period was over, Vladimir Petrov easily tapped a Boris Mikhailov rebound past an off-balance Dryden. At the end of the first period the score was tied 2–2.

Team Canada couldn't believe the

shape the Soviets players were in. During the first intermission, Henderson sat on the dressing room bench trying to catch his breath. During the first period he had gasped for air, while the Soviets never showed signs of getting tired. They kept up to the Canadians stride for stride. Team Canada realized they were in for a battle.

People were still in shock as the second period started. Team Canada wasn't as good as everyone had thought. Even worse, the Soviets were much better than anyone had imagined. Team Canada tried to get back into the game. The Soviets didn't fold under the pressure. They just wouldn't quit.

The second period was only two and a half minutes old when the Soviets struck. Alexander Maltsev, deep in his own end, passed the puck forward to a speeding linemate. Streaking with the puck down the right side was Valeri Kharlamov. He

The Russians were known as a finesse hockey team. But they didn't back down when the play got physical. They weren't going to be pushed around.

stood at only five-foot-six and weighed 154 pounds. He was a blur with the puck. He skated past his own blue line, the centre line, and then the Canadian blue line. He raced toward Team Canada defencemen Don Awrey and Rod Seiling. Kharlamov dipped his left shoulder. The defencemen thought he would try and skate through them. Instead, he smoothly moved to the outside and around Awrey. A beaten Awrey turned and lunged for the puck. It was too late. Kharlamov shot the puck between Ken Dryden's legs and into the net.

Team Canada was stunned by what had happened.

Less than eight minutes later, Kharlamov made another rush. He collected a loose puck off a faceoff just outside the Russian blue line. He streaked across the ice at incredible speed, and once again faced defencemen Awrey and Seiling. In an instant he raised his stick in the air and unleashed a powerful slapshot. Dryden didn't have time to react to the blast. It blew past him and into the net.

After the Russian goals, a strange sound was heard in the arena. People in the crowd began to boo Team Canada. They did not like the score. They also didn't like how Team Canada turned to playing rough, dirty hockey. Nobody applauded as the second period ended.

Team Canada forward Bobby Clarke scored to open the third period. But Team Canada was tired and didn't have the energy to contain the Russians. Five minutes later, Boris Mikhailov scored to give the Russians another two-goal lead. They scored another two goals before the game ended. The best players in the NHL had been beaten 7–3. The Canadians lost at their own game in their own country.

The Canadian players were in awe

of what they had seen. It was painfully clear that Tretiak was not the horrible goaltender everyone had been led to believe. The Soviets were highly skilled players. Their play ended all hopes for a Team Canada sweep.

Canada had judged Russia without much thought. Ability makes a team, not the quality of their helmets, skates, or jerseys. At the Soviet pre-series practice, Team Canada had laughed at the Russian team. After Game One, nobody in Canada was laughing. They now saw the series as a war to be won.

8 Fighting Back

At first, Russian hockey officials told their team to try not to lose by a lot. After the first game in the Summit Series, the Russians were sent new directions from Moscow. Now it was the players' duty to win all remaining games.

After the Game One loss, Team Canada felt more pressure to win. They were playing in front of a doubting nation. Coach Sinden realized he needed to make changes. He had to find the right team chemistry to win. He changed the lineup for the second game.

Only one Team Canada forward line stayed intact for Game Two. Sinden kept together the Paul Henderson, Bobby Clarke, and Ron Ellis line. They were a line of physical players that could score goals. Sinden sat some of the team's skilled goal scorers, replacing them with much more physical players like J.P. Parise. They were not All-Star NHL players. They weren't goal-scoring threats. Instead, they liked to bodycheck. Sinden thought this would throw the Russians off their game.

The second game of the series was played in Toronto at Maple Leaf Gardens. A sold-out crowd of 16,485 filled the rink. They wanted to see Canada win. After Game One they didn't know what would happen.

As the game started, the Soviets saw that the Canadians' attitudes had changed.

They had a new respect for the Russian athletes. The Canadian players were also more focused on the game.

Team Canada knew they had to shut down the Russian attack. Canada played a more physical game. They checked hard along the boards and in the corners. They threw their weight around. Sinden's plan threw the Russian players off their game. The set-pass pattern that worked in the

Team Canada center Bobby Clarke did not hold back against the Russians. His greatest battle was against Russian star Valeri Kharlamov (Number 17).

first game never got started. Plays that clicked so well in Game One failed in Game Two. They were not used to worrying about getting their heads knocked off. The Russian attack was almost totally shut down. What did get through was stopped by Team Canada goalie Tony Esposito.

The Canadians played a more controlled game. They were flawless in their defensive zone. They hit the Soviets with thundering bodychecks. It was not a popular plan, but it worked.

Tony O

Tony Esposito and his brother Phil grew up in Sault Ste. Marie, Ontario. Tony rose to fame with the Chicago Black Hawks. He was one of the pioneers of the butterfly style of goaltending. He won a Stanley Cup and three Vezina trophies over his 16-year career. He was voted into the Hockey Hall of Fame in 1988.

The first period was bruising for the Russians. They couldn't score against Team Canada, but Canada couldn't score against Russia either. By the end of the period they held a scoreless tie.

Team Canada opened the scoring in the second period. Phil Esposito was battling for the puck in the Soviet end. He freed it from the skates of a Soviet defender. He swung the puck from his backhand to his forehand and shot from the slot, beating the helpless Russian goaltender.

Team Canada held their 1–0 lead going into the third period.

On a Team Canada power play, just 1:19 into the final period, Canada was desperate to double their score. Defenceman Brad Park burst out of the Canadian end with the puck. Hitting centre ice, he quickly glanced up to see Yvan Cournoyer. He fired the puck directly onto the stick of his teammate. Cournoyer was on a breakaway as he skated around the Soviet defencemen. There was nobody between him and the goalie. He smoothly tucked a shot between the pads of Vladislav Tretiak. Team Canada now led 2–0.

Just a few minutes later, Russia broke through the Canadian defence. This time, Tony Esposito couldn't make the save. Russia scored to give Team Canada only a one-goal lead.

The Soviets got the advantage when Canada took a penalty. The Russians moved the puck around. They were looking for the perfect chance to tie the game. It felt like they would score.

But as they came toward the Canadian net, the Soviets lost the puck. Team Canada defenceman Guy Lapointe tried to clear the puck out of the Canadian zone. The Soviets stopped it from being cleared, but it bounced to Esposito. With his back to the play, he blindly threw the puck out past the Canadian blue line.

The puck landed on the stick of Peter Mahovlich. Only one Soviet defender stood between Peter and a chance to score on Tretiak.

With long strides, Peter moved the puck toward centre ice. He spotted an opening and made his move. When he got to the blue line, he faked a slapshot. He then stepped to his right and went around the Russian defenceman. Peter was just steps from the goal, alone, one on one. Tretiak slid down to the ice and stacked his pads to create a wall. Peter shot at the goal. Somehow he found a crack and scored. The Toronto crowd exploded in one great cheer. Tretiak was in shock.

Peter's brother Frank finished the scoring for Team Canada. They held their lead and won the game 4–1.

The Soviets now faced a different Team Canada. Team Canada rose to defend their country's honour. The victory restored a nation's pride. People forgot about the nightmare in Montreal.

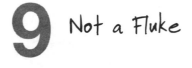

9 Not a Fluke

Was Canada still the number one hockey country in the world? That was the question Team Canada wanted to answer in Game Three. Nobody would doubt them again if they continued to win like they had in Toronto.

The third game was played in Winnipeg on September 6. That city didn't have an NHL team yet. The Winnipeg Jets played in the rival World Hockey Association (WHA). The Jets' newest star was former

Chicago Black Hawk Bobby Hull. He was one of Canada's best players. But he was not allowed on Team Canada. Since the NHL helped organize the series, only NHL players were allowed to join the national team.

Team Canada didn't want to tamper with a winning combination. Only one roster change was made for the third game. The roster was always decided on a day-to-day basis. The original promise to play everybody was set aside.

Some fans thought forward J.P. Parise shouldn't have been on the team. They couldn't believe he was given a chance to play. But he had showed his value in the second game. His bodychecks changed how the Russians played.

In the third game, Parise opened the scoring at 1:54 of the first period. Defenceman Bill White shot the puck at the Soviet net from the blue line. It rebounded off Tretiak's pads and right onto Parise's stick. He shot once but Tretiak made the save. Then a second chance got it past the Russian goaltender.

Team Canada couldn't hold the lead for long. The Russians soon scored to tie the game. But before the period was over, Team Canada forward Jean Ratelle regained the lead for Canada. He converted a perfect pass from Cournoyer into a goal. At the end of the first period, Team Canada was winning 2–1.

Captain Phil Esposito scored at the 4:19 mark of the second period. Then, midway through that period, the Soviets trimmed that lead to 3–2. Just 51 seconds later, forward Paul Henderson used his speed to win a footrace with Soviet defenceman Alexander Gusev. Henderson picked up the puck and scored.

Ahead by two, everything seemed right in Canada's hockey world. For the moment, the loss in Montreal was a distant memory. But the team was tired and the Soviets kept coming strong. Harry Sinden's fears were soon realized.

The Russians had a reserve of fresh young legs ready to jump into the game. The Soviet coach gave some action to their "Kid Line" of Yuri Lebedev, Alexander Bodunov, and Vyacheslav Anisin. They were three university students. They increased the speed of the game. They drove into the Team Canada zone with an unstoppable attack.

"I didn't know what university they had been attending, but they must have majored in hockey," wrote reporter Jim Coleman.

Canada led 4–2 when the youthful Soviets hit the ice. Together they scored two goals in less than four minutes.

The game was tied 4–4 going into the final period. Like the last game, the

The Greatest

Vladislav Tretiak is considered one of the greatest goaltenders of all time. He was the best-known player on the Soviet Union's national hockey team. The Soviet government blocked any NHL clubs from drafting him. He won ten World Championships and three Olympic gold medals. In 1989, Tretiak was the first non-NHL player to be elected into the Hockey Hall of Fame.

Canadians were very tired by the third period. The Russians controlled the play. Twenty-year-old goalie Vladislav Tretiak continued to frustrate Team Canada.

Every shift was a battle. Team Canada was just holding on to the tie.

"In Winnipeg, they finally understood they had to deal with amateurs who could play hockey at this level," said Alexander Yakushev.

The Canadians successfully held off the Soviet attack. They even had one good chance to take the lead.

Speedy Canadian winger Paul Henderson broke in alone on Tretiak. He made a shot that looked as if it would go over Tretiak's shoulder and into the net. Henderson thought he had scored. He even had his stick up in the air to signal a goal. But to his amazement, Tretiak snatched the puck out of the air. The Russian goalie came up with the puck and preserved the 4–4 tie. Henderson couldn't believe what had happened.

The tied score held until the final whistle. The two teams were at a deadlock in the series standings.

"The Russians compare with any team in the NHL," said coach Sinden. "Anybody in this country who thinks we're not playing a great hockey team is crazy."

The Soviet coaches had their own discovery.

"We thought the Canadian team would be stronger," said Russian coach Vsevolod Bobrov.

"We came to Canada with the illusion about Canadian hockey pros," said assistant coach Boris Kulagin. "After the three games that have been held so far, we've discovered they are ordinary people like ourselves."

The Russians were not happy about Team Canada's poor play. Neither was the Canadian public. The Team Canada players were about to learn first-hand how their fans felt about them.

10 Abandoned

Canadian support of Team Canada was not very strong at this point. A tied series wasn't good enough for them. Fans thought the best of the NHL should win everything. The Russians' brilliant play in the first three games didn't change their minds. Team Canada was supposed to win easily.

Coach Sinden made more changes to the lineup. He was still looking for the right combination of players. The fans questioned whether Sinden knew what he was doing. Sinden had a hard time knowing what was right. He started to question his own decisions.

Canadian pride was hurt. Team Canada had trouble competing against the Soviets on their own ice. The Soviets appeared to be the better team. They were able to handle whatever came at them.

"We dispelled the myth about the unbeatable Canadian professionals," said Vladimir Petrov. "And after Game Four in North America, there was no myth anymore."

The fourth game of the series was played in Vancouver on September 8. It took only two minutes before Team Canada experienced just how upset the Canadian public was with their performance in the series. Over 15,000 unhappy fans at the Pacific Coliseum vented their anger.

The first target of the fans' wrath was

Bill Goldsworthy. At 1:24 into the first period, the big Canadian winger was given the first of two minor penalties. Both penalties ended with goals from Soviet centre Boris Mikhailov.

The Soviets' first goal arrived at 2:01. Soon, boos were heard coming from the crowd. With the second goal at 7:29, the booing got louder. The crowd was upset with Team Canada and they wanted the players to know it.

At the end of the first period, the Soviets led 2–0.

Between periods, Sinden decided to give speedy Gilbert Perreault more ice time. The coach hoped Perreault's fast skating might create a chance or two. At worst, he could at least keep up with the Soviets.

Early in the second period, Sinden's decision proved wise. Perreault scored a beautiful goal off an electrifying end-to-end rush.

Alexander Maltsev played top-level hockey from 1967 to 1984, and won two Olympic gold medals. His 213 career goals in international play are the most by any Soviet player.

But the buzz created by Perreault's exciting goal was short-lived. The Soviets restored their two-goal lead just 57 seconds later.

The Team Canada defenders couldn't seem to clear their zone against the Soviets.

On one play, Alexander Maltsev dug the puck off the boards and passed it out to Kharlamov in the slot. But Kharlamov didn't take the shot. He spotted teammate Vladimir Vikulov standing alone beside the Canadian goal. Kharlamov backhanded a pass to him that Vikulov one-timed past goalie Ken Dryden.

At the end of two periods, the Soviets were ahead 4–1. And the booing from the crowd got even louder. Fans weren't just angry that Team Canada was losing the game. They also didn't like how the team was playing.

Winning wasn't good enough for some fans. They wanted the team to show the entire world that Canada was superior at hockey. But the bad penalties and rough, dirty play made Team Canada look bad. People were more impressed by the skilled play of the Soviets.

Phil Esposito and Paul Henderson sat

next to each other during the second intermission. Both were unhappy with their own play. But it was the Canadian fans that worried them most.

"Our own people are turning on us," said Henderson to Esposito.

"I hope I'm picked the star of the game," Esposito replied, "because I'm really going to give them a piece of my mind tonight. I've had enough of this."

Team Canada opened the scoring in the third period. But at 11:05, Vladimir Shadrin put the game out of reach. He broke the Canadians' spirits by sliding the puck past Dryden for their fifth goal. With just 22 seconds remaining, Canadian forward Dennis Hull scored. But Team Canada didn't have time to score another.

The final score was Soviet Union 5, Team Canada 3. The series was half over. The Soviets seemed to be in complete control with a 2-1-1 record.

After the final whistle, the booing got even louder. People across Canada were booing at their team.

Team Canada captain Phil Esposito couldn't believe his ears. His anger had started when he heard the first boo at the start of the game. For three periods he had listened to the crowd booing his team. But Phil played so well that he got his wish. As Team Canada's game star he would be interviewed for National television. He would also be heard in the Vancouver arena.

When Esposito was named game star, the chorus of boos grew louder. The crowd got even louder as he skated the length of the ice to be interviewed. He was ready.

He stood beside television reporter Johnny Esaw to be interviewed. Fans were yelling at Phil. They were throwing things at him. Phil just stood there with sweat pouring down his face. The anger that had built up over three periods could be seen in his eyes. What he was going to say would strike the heart of every member on the team.

"To the people across Canada — we tried, we gave it our best. And to the people that boo us, geez, all of us guys are really disheartened and we're disappointed . . . We cannot believe the bad press we've got, the booing we've gotten in our own buildings . . . We're trying, I mean, we're doing the best we can. But they've got a good team, let's face facts.

"I tell ya, every one of us thirty-five guys that came out and played for Team Canada, we did it because we love our country, and not for any other reason. No other reason. And I don't think it's fair that we should be booed."

Esposito's words lifted the spirits of his team, but the fans were still unhappy with the Canadian players. Only a small crowd was at the airport to send off Team Canada. The team felt abandoned.

"When we left Vancouver, we were determined to do whatever was humanly possible to win the series," said winger Dennis Hull. "We wanted to show these people that we could do it."

11 Becoming the Real Team Canada

It was Russia's game after the most disappointing week in Canadian sports history. In just seven days, the Russians had destroyed the 100-year-old myth of Canadian hockey superiority. They also ended the 50-year-old legend of NHL invincibility.

"I'm ready to believe anything," said forward Frank Mahovlich. "After seeing what the Russian hockey players did to us at our game, I'm afraid nothing in sport is sacred anymore."

"They were so skilled," said forward Paul Henderson. "Their skill level was unnerving. They had a game plan. They passed the puck constantly. It was all about controlling the puck, while we were much more about shooting the puck in, going to get it, crashing and banging the boards. They never thought about doing that. They never wanted to give the puck up."

In less than 20 years, the Russians had gone from an unknown to a world hockey power. During that time, Canadian hockey had not changed at all.

"I don't understand it," said Team Canada coach Harry Sinden. "Twelve and fifteen years ago Canada beat Russia with guys who hauled lunch buckets all week. Guys who delivered milk. Guys who tended bars. Why can't these guys we have here — the highest paid players in the world — beat them?"

Team Canada's so-called stars had been total busts. Except for the Esposito brothers, the non-stars were the best players. People like J.P. Parise, Bobby Clarke, and Paul Henderson outplayed superstars like Vic Hadfield. During the previous NHL season, Hadfield had scored 50 goals. He quit Team Canada when he was replaced by unknown left-winger J.P. Parise.

"Parise came here and worked," Sinden

The Flin Flon Bomber

During the Summit Series, Bobby Clarke was a 22-year-old forward who played for the Philadelphia Flyers. The Flin Flon, Manitoba, native was just starting his career. He eventually became one of the top players in the NHL. He led the Flyers to Stanley Cup championships in 1974 and 1975. The three-time league MVP award winner was inducted into the Hockey Hall of Fame in 1987.

said. "Hadfield didn't."

The Summit Series wasn't going as planned. It became much more than just a series of hockey games. Canada's heritage was being ruined. For some of the players, it had started out as a fun series. After four games, the series became a war. Now all that mattered was thrashing the Soviets.

The Canadian players didn't have much desire to board the plane for Europe. After being in the spotlight for a month, they felt forgotten.

"By the time we left Canada we felt like we had been literally deserted," said Sinden.

To Canadians, it didn't matter that the Soviets had proven themselves a worthy opponent. The fans didn't want reasons. They wanted results. In the eyes of the fans, Team Canada had played badly. They felt Team Canada had let them down by not upholding the honour of their country.

"When we went over there, it seemed like everybody was against us, but I think that brought us all a lot closer together as a team," said Parise. "That week, we went out and we knew what we had to do to win. We had to upgrade our conditioning, but we were also finally getting to know each other."

In the 1970s, NHL players didn't have friends on other teams. But as members of Team Canada, they started to put aside their old NHL loyalties and personal rivalries. The Canadian players began to bond. They felt they were in this battle together.

The players' spirits were lifted when they reached Moscow. They had not been abandoned by everyone after all. Their wives, team officials, and 2,700 Canadian hockey fans greeted them when they arrived. The fans had paid thousands of dollars to spend a week in Moscow, support their team, and witness history.

Team Canada did not feel so alone going into the fifth game in Moscow. But would it be enough to drive them to victory in the series?

12 War on Ice

Canada and the Soviet Union were fighting a war on ice. Hockey supremacy was at stake. It was a lot of pressure for both teams to be under. Team Canada found it even worse with Russia ahead by two games in the series.

But as each day before the fifth game passed, the Canadians' confidence grew. It helped that their attitude toward the Russians had changed.

"They reconstructed their thoughts and

The real battle began in Moscow for Game Four. Team Canada was ready to fight till the end to regain its national pride.

attitudes to us, the Soviet team," said Vladimir Petrov. "They started treating us like equals."

The Soviets were confident going into the fifth game on September 22. The last four games would be played in Moscow's Luzhniki Arena. The capacity was 15,000 people. A ticket to a game cost almost a month's salary for the average person living in Moscow. It was estimated that

50 million people across the Soviet Union would watch the game on television.

The Soviets wondered how they could possibly do any worse on home ice. They would play before their home fans and with European referees. They thought Team Canada would be at a great disadvantage.

But the Canadian players felt strangely at home. They knew that they had about 2,700 fans in the stands. And the Canadian public back home was rallying behind the team.

"We had received at least 10,000 telegrams from people back home wishing us good luck," said Team Canada defenceman Brad Park. "So we taped all the telegrams to the walls in the dressing room, so that every time we went to practice or went out for a period we would see all these telegrams." Team Canada finally felt the support of their country going into Game Five.

Team Canada's mood was lifted even more at the start of the game. The two teams lined up at their own blue lines for the playing of both national anthems. "O Canada" was belted out with greater volume and emotion than the Soviet anthem. The 2,700 Canadians in attendance sung the loudest anthem they had ever heard. Many of the players joined in the singing, too.

Those Canadian fans had a lot to cheer about in the first two periods.

Winger J.P. Parise scored in the first period. Then, just 2:36 into the second period, centre Bobby Clarke added to the Canadian score. After winning a faceoff in the Soviet zone, he passed the puck over to Paul Henderson. Clarke then moved into the slot and Henderson passed it back. Clarke barged toward the goal with the puck on his stick and snuck a backhand shot between Tretiak's legs. Midway through the second period, Henderson also tapped in a rebound in to put Canada ahead by three goals!

Everything seemed to be going right for Team Canada. They were in complete control of the game. Tony Esposito had stopped all 22 shots he had faced. At the end of two periods, Canada was ahead 3–0.

Team Canada's play had improved greatly during the two weeks between games. It really looked as if they had come together on the ice. The potential of their team was finally being reached.

"You could see everyone was working hard. There was much more intensity. We hadn't had that feeling since the first day of training camp. It really felt like we were finally a team. The emotion was finally there," said coach Sinden.

It seemed like the Soviets were beaten. But they weren't out yet.

The Soviets scored early in the third period. Winger Yuri Blinov broke Tony Esposito's shutout. But Team Canada didn't waver. Less than two minutes later, Henderson took a pass from Clarke and restored Canada's three-goal lead.

But the Russians could not be held down for much longer. Team Canada couldn't protect their lead. In a shocking five-and-a-half minutes, the Soviets were back in the game.

The comeback began at 9:05 with Vyacheslav Anisin redirecting a Yuri Liapkin pass into Esposito's net. Eight seconds later, Vladimir Shadrin completed a nifty three-way passing play for a second goal. And at 11:49, Alexander Gusev tied the game by beating Esposito with a high shot into the corner.

"When they came back, it didn't shock us the way it did in the first game, because we knew it was possible," said Yvan Cournoyer.

Yevgeny Zimin played eight seasons with the Russian National Team. His career ended with the 1972 Summit Series.

The comeback was complete with a little more than five minutes left in the game. Team Canada forward Bobby Clarke made a big error. While coming out of his own zone, he decided to pass the puck behind him to a defenceman. It never reached its intended target. Russian Vladimir Vikulov snatched up the puck. He was alone in front of the Canadian goal. Coming from the left of the net, Vikulov skated right across the goalmouth. He drew Team Canada netminder Tony Esposito out of position. Then Vikulov slipped a backhander around him for the go-ahead goal. The Soviet National Team now led 5–4.

Tony Esposito felt that he had let the team down. Canada tried to come back, but Tretiak stopped any scoring chances. The Soviets won the game 5–4. They were certain now that they would win the whole series.

When Team Canada left the ice that day, they were shocked and angry. But the Canadian fans in the stands quickly lifted their spirits. They gave Team Canada a standing ovation. It sent the players the message: "You're still our boys, you're still great, and we still back you." It was uplifting for the team to know they were not alone. Their fans would cheer them on no matter how the series ended.

Team Canada now needed three wins in the final three games, all on Moscow ice, to take the series. They could have seen this as an impossible task. But the Canadians still thought they could win. They knew they still had a chance to show

Canada was tops in hockey.

"I don't think anybody except the team believed we could win the series at that point," said Cournoyer. "It was an awfully tall order, but we really did believe we would do it."

13 Staying Alive

Team Canada couldn't afford to lose the sixth game. The stress they were under was unbelievable. But they were confident. One factor Team Canada had in its favour was experience. They were used to playing in the intense, pressure-filled NHL playoffs.

They also had the excitement of their fans to keep them going. When the players felt down, they could just read the many telegrams they received and remember the fans back home. They could also look up into the Moscow stands full of red and white maple leafs.

Team Canada had to adjust how they played during the series. The Soviets had discovered ways to get to the Canadians. They found success and stuck to it. But the Canadian players were always adapting and experimenting with new things. They kept looking for ways to break through the Soviet mastery they showed early in the series.

The most notable change was made in Game Six. Team Canada was now able to break up the Soviet passing plays. The Canadian players skated with the Russians to intercept their criss-crossing plays in the neutral zone. And they returned to backchecking, holding the blue line with determination. The Russians didn't adapt.

Right from the start of the game, the Soviets swarmed into the Canadian zone.

Team Canada was tested like never before. They swarmed right back.

The Canadian players were clearly sharper on defence. They intercepted Soviet passes and swiftly made the change to an offensive attack. Team Canada goalie Ken Dryden was nervous about starting the game. He didn't like how he had played in his first two starts. But he was strong in net this time. In a five-minute span, he pushed back every Soviet attack. He kicked out Yuri Liapkin's hard slapshot from the point. He made a pad save on a dangerous drive by Alexander Maltsev from in close. He caught Vladimir Vikulov's rising shot out of the air. Dryden's reflexes were back. With each save, he felt his confidence building. Along with it grew his teammates' faith in him.

The first period ended with neither team scoring.

Very early in the second period, Dryden faced a two-on-one. Alexander Yakushev broke out with Alexandre Volchkov. He shot the puck, but it went wide. Vladimir Shadrin trailed on the play. He picked up the rebound and got it back to Liapkin on the point. Heavily screened, Dryden didn't see Liapkin's slapshot until the puck was in the net. The Soviets took a one-goal lead.

The Canadians' confidence never wavered. They were playing well. The team dominated the game for the next few minutes. Dennis Hull and Yvan Cournoyer both scored to give Team Canada a 2–1 lead.

The Canadians' goals were scored in less than a minute. The Soviets didn't know what had happened. Seconds later, a normally steady Vladimir Lutchenko made a blind back-pass out of his zone to centre ice. Paul Henderson intercepted it and skated into the Russian end. He got around the Soviet defencemen and released a quick slapshot low to the ice. Taken by surprise, Tretiak didn't even move as the puck slid past him. Canada now led 3–1.

The Canadians wanted to hold on to their lead at any cost.

"My view of it is this, I don't care how we win as long as we win," said assistant coach John Ferguson.

During the first intermission, Ferguson told Bobby Clarke to get Valeri Kharlamov out of the game. Kharlamov was the most dangerous Russian player. He was a scoring threat

Valeri Kharlamov was seen as Team Canada's greatest threat during the Summit Series, until he was injured by Bobby Clarke in Game Six.

National Hero

Valeri Kharlamov was once considered one of the greatest hockey players in the world. He was an eight-time winner of the World Hockey Championship and two-time Olympic gold medal winner. Valeri was only 33 years old when he died in a car crash. He was inducted into the Hall of Fame in 2005.

whenever he was on the ice. Getting him out of the lineup increased Team Canada's chances of winning. Clarke never questioned his assignment.

In the second period, Clarke swung his stick like an axe against Kharlamov's ankle. The Russian's ankle was fractured. Kharlamov finished playing Game Six, but missed Game Seven altogether. He was back on the ice for Game Eight, but after his injury, he was no longer a threat to the Canadian team.

A combination of stellar defensive play

and excellent work by Dryden in goal helped Team Canada to keep their lead. By the end of the game, they had won 3–2.

Team Canada was still alive in the series. They never gave up. The players showed they would do whatever was needed to win. Only two games remained. The Russians didn't think they could lose.

The seventh game on September 26 was a battle going into the final minutes. The game was tied 3–3 in the third period. A tie would give the Russians the series.

With two minutes left, Canadian winger Paul Henderson provided the heroics for his team. He got the puck at centre ice and rushed rapidly into the Russians' defensive zone. Two Russian defenders were between him and the goal.

Henderson deked his way around them. Speed and strength brought him face to face with Tretiak. Henderson lost his balance and started to fall to the ice. But as Henderson fell, he shot the puck. The puck squeezed between Tretiak's arm and his body to score. This was Henderson's sixth goal of the series. Team Canada won the seventh game 4–3.

Team Canada had shown their ability to fight hard. They were all devoted to the single goal of winning, from the first second to the last of Game Seven. They were playing more like the Russians. They were working like a team.

The Summit Series battle had come down to one final game.

14 Deadlock

Most of Canada stood still on September 28, 1972. It was the eighth and final game of the Summit Series. The game was played at night in Moscow. Due to the time difference, the game was televised during the day in Canada. People skipped work to watch the game. School principals cancelled classes at their schools. Televisions were set up for all the teachers and students to watch the game in their classrooms. Most Canadians who were alive at that time still know where they were when Game Eight was played.

The series began with Canada having high hopes for an easy victory. After seven games, however, those thoughts had long since vanished. The Soviets had proven themselves worthy opponents. By this last game they were about as close as two teams could get. They were 60 minutes away from settling the issue of which country was world's best in hockey.

Canada got into trouble early. Bill White and Peter Mahovlich were both given penalties in the first three minutes of play. With the penalty box loaded up, the Soviets opened the scoring. Big winger Alexander Yakushev parked himself in front of the Canadian goal and snapped a rebound past goalie Ken Dryden.

Less than two minutes later, things got worse for Canada. Winger J.P. Parise was given an interference penalty for bumping

Russian player Alexander Yakuskev was often overshadowed by Kharlamov. By the end of the Summit Series, he lead the Soviets in scoring with seven goals and four assists.

Alexander Maltsev. Parise didn't think it was worthy of a penalty. He slammed his stick on the ice and yelled at the referee. The referee gave him an additional ten-minute penalty. It looked like Parise was going to hit the referee with his stick, but he didn't. He was still kicked out of the game.

It could have gotten worse for Team Canada. But a few minutes later, a Russian player was issued a penalty. Team Canada put pressure on the Russians in their zone. Brad Park took a shot on Vladislav Tretiak. The goalie saved it, but the puck rebounded out to Phil Esposito, who slammed the puck into the Russian net to tie the game.

Midway through the period, defenceman Vladimir Lutchenko regained the Soviet lead. Dryden was screened by a group of players. He was helpless when Lutchenko shot the puck and couldn't make the save. Russia 2, Canada 1.

But before the first period was over, Canada drew even again. Brad Park scored on a nice passing play with help from Dennis Hull and Jean Ratelle.

"You know in a game like that anything can happen," said Coach Sinden. "But we were certain we could beat them and were interested on making it awfully tough on them."

Now, after 27 days, seven games, and one period, the series was still even. Just 40 minutes remained.

Just 21 seconds into the second period, the Soviets stunned the Canadians with another goal.

Unlike North American rinks, the Luzhinki Arena was not equipped with plastic glass around the boards and behind the net. Instead, the area behind the net was made of huge sheets of springy wire mesh. Russian Yakushev drifted a shot high off the mesh. It sprung back out toward the blue line. Vladimir Shadrin found the puck and drove it behind a startled Dryden.

Sensing they could put the Canadians away, the Soviets pressed hard to expand their lead. But Dryden was excellent in Team Canada's goal, and the Canadian players continued to battle back into the Russian end. Midway through the period,

The Student

Ken Dryden originally picked law school over professional hockey. He joined the Montreal Canadiens after the school year finished in the spring of 1971. He led them to a Stanley Cup championship. He would backstop the Canadiens to another six championships over an eight-season career. In such a short time, he also won five Vezina trophies as the league's top goaltender. He was inducted into the Hockey Hall of Fame in 1983.

White snuck down the right side from the point. He received a pass from Rod Gilbert and scored.

But the Soviets continued to pressure the Canadiens. This time, Team Canada could not defend themselves. Two minutes after White's goal, Soviet winger Yakushev scored their fourth goal. Another Team Canada penalty with four minutes left in the period led to the Soviets' fifth goal.

At the end of two periods, the Soviets

Alexander Yakushev played with the Russian National team from 1965 to 1979. He was inducted into the IIHF Hall of Fame in 2003.

led Team Canada 5–3.

Still, there was no panic in the Canadians' dressing room between periods. The players remained calm. There wasn't a negative thought. They still had the opportunity to make their country proud.

History would be made in the next period. It was up to Team Canada to determine what was written.

15  The Goal

It would have been easy for Team Canada to quit. They were down two goals with only 20 minutes left in the final game. There would be no overtime and no ninth game. This was it. The Canadians had to score three goals and stop any Soviets from scoring.

Team Canada knew they still had an opportunity to make their country proud. And the Soviets knew Canada would fight to the end with everything they had.

As the final period began, Team Canada burst out with a blazing offensive attack. Bobby Clarke won the opening faceoff. Ron Ellis powered a shot from the blue line that Tretiak had to hold onto for dear life. If he gave up a rebound, Clarke or Henderson would be sure to scoop it up and score.

The Canadian players were primed. But so were the Soviets. Yakushev and Vyacheslav Anisin broke out on a two-on-one in the Canadian zone. Dryden made a fine save on Anisin's hard shot. The Soviets created some tense moments, but shot wide of the net three times.

Team Canada's big line was made up of Phil Esposito, Yvan Cournoyer, and Frank Mahovlich. But for the final period, Sinden switched one brother for the other. He took Frank off the line and replaced him with Peter.

At one point, Peter Mahovlich made a

superstar, all-out, end-to-end rush. From behind his own net, Peter passed up to Cournoyer. Cournoyer returned the puck to Peter, who battled all the way up the boards. He ended up in the corner to the right of the Soviet net. A Soviet player skated toward him and laid a bodycheck on him. But as Peter fell to the ice, he got off a pass to Esposito. The puck struck a Soviet's stick in front of the net and flipped into the air. Esposito batted it out of the air and down to his feet. He swung at the puck on the ice, but missed. On his second swing, he connected. The puck flew through the air, between Tretiak's pads, and into the net. Canadian fans around the world erupted in delight. Team Canada had cut the Russian lead to one goal, 5–4. They still had time to win the game.

At the ten-minute mark, Sinden noticed something that gave him new hope for victory. The Soviets were falling back into a defensive game. They were trying to protect the lead instead of adding to it. It was the first time in the series that the Soviets had done this. It was not how the Soviet team played hockey. Abandoning Anatoli Tarasov's attacking style became their undoing.

Esposito's line took the faceoff in the Canadian end. Phil won the faceoff and got the puck back to defenceman Brad Park. He carried the puck behind his own net, then moved swiftly away from the Soviet players and up the left boards. He threaded a long, rink-wide pass back to Esposito. With four Soviets in close pursuit, Esposito carried the puck over the blue line. He cut into the open. Then he let go a chest-high shot 15 feet from the goal. Tretiak blocked the shot, but it bobbled back into play.

Esposito regained the puck. This time

three Soviet players surrounded him. But none of them could knock the puck away from him. Esposito was doing everything he could to get the puck out to another Team Canada player. His first effort was swept back by Tretiak. His second effort came out to Cournoyer, who took a shot instantly. Tretiak made the save, but dropped the puck. Both Esposito and Cournoyer lunged for the puck in a mad scramble. Cournoyer got there first. He floated a backhander over Tretiak and into the net.

The Roadrunner

Yvan Cournoyer was nicknamed "The Roadrunner" for his blinding speed. He won ten Stanley Cup championships as a member of the Montreal Canadiens. He finished his career with 428 goals and 863 points. He was inducted into the Hockey Hall of Fame in 1982.

The game was tied 5–5. If the game ended in a tie, the total series wouldn't be tied. The win would go to the team that had scored the most goals. The Russians would edge Team Canada and declare victory. Team Canada had to score another goal to win the series.

With seven minutes and four seconds of playing time remaining, the Soviets suddenly came out of their defensive shell. Both sides were on the attack looking for the series-deciding goal.

Gary Bergman had a good scoring chance, but Tretiak kicked it out. Moments late, a Soviet player carried the puck over the Canadian blue line. He tried to carry it behind Park and Guy Lapointe, but they bodychecked him into the air.

Now there was less than one minute to play. The Esposito, Cournoyer, and Peter Mahovlich line was nearing the end of a shift. Coach Sinden decided he wanted fresh players for the final push. He called for the Henderson, Ellis, and Clarke line to take the ice. They might have one last chance to score.

Henderson yelled at Peter to come off the ice. Peter didn't hesitate and came right to the bench. As he came off the ice, Henderson vaulted over the boards. He thought he could score, but time was running out.

They tried to get Cournoyer off the ice, too. He even started to head for the bench, but then he said to himself, "No, I'm going to give it one more shot." He stayed on the ice.

Esposito stayed on the ice as well. He thought, "There isn't any way in the world I'm going off now." He felt a goal was coming and he wanted to be in on it.

A Soviet defenceman got the puck behind his net. He shot it around the boards, hoping to clear it out of his zone.

But Cournoyer was standing right there to get the puck. He saw Henderson streaking down the far wing. Cournoyer passed to Henderson, but the puck went behind him. Henderson reached for the puck but was hooked by a Russian player and crashed into the end boards. The puck went into the corner. Three Soviet players were there, but none of them picked up the puck. Esposito broke through and snagged it. Without hesitation, he shot at Tretiak. The Soviet goalie blocked the shot easily with his stick. But he allowed a rebound.

Henderson had scrambled to his feet. He picked up the rebound and was alone in front of Tretiak. Henderson took the shot. Tretiak made a pad save and sprawled on his back. Again the puck came out to Henderson. He shot again. It was a low slider aimed straight at the narrow space between Tretiak's body and the right

The Goal Scorer

Paul Henderson wasn't a superstar in the NHL, but his Summit Series performance made him into a Canadian legend. Over the eight-game series, he scored seven goals. His scoring touch won three of the games for Team Canada. He played 13 seasons in the NHL with Detroit, Toronto, and Atlanta. His best season was 1971–72, when he scored 38 goals for the Toronto Maple Leafs.

post. The puck slid into the net, and the Canadians had scored!

Tretiak was still lying flat on his back as Henderson raised his arms and stick into the air. He leaped into Cournoyer's arms. Team Canada's bench cleared to congratulate Henderson and celebrate the goal. In the stands, 2,700 Canadians stood up and cheered. Back in Canada, a nation celebrated.

But another 34 seconds remained in the game. The Soviets could still score. Sinden sent out his best defensive players. They didn't let the Soviets anywhere near Dryden.

Canadian fans in Moscow roared out

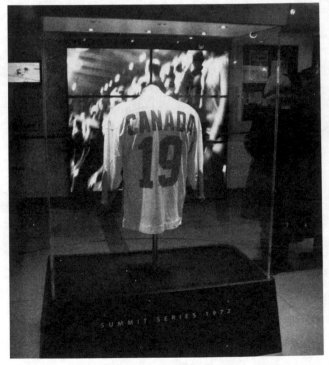

Paul Henderson's Team Canada jersey is one of the most popular pieces of Canadian hockey history. The jersey recently sold for one million dollars.

the countdown of the final seconds of the game. When the final buzzer sounded, Canada reclaimed its honour. They had won the game 6–5. Team Canada won the Summit Series with a 4-3-1 record. The Soviets were silenced by Canada's victory.

The old questions had been answered. Canada's best players could defeat the Soviets' best players. For now, Canada was on top again. Every year the battle between these two hockey-loving nations would continue. But they would never recreate the excitement of this series in September 1972.

Epilogue

The 1972 Summit Series changed hockey. The Soviet and Canadian styles of hockey would eventually mix, and a new style of hockey would be created. The NHL players were impressed by the Russians' conditioning. They saw the emphasis on skill over brute strength. It's the style of hockey played in the NHL today. But that change came slowly.

When the NHL pros weren't playing on Team Canada, the Russians dominated world hockey. For the following twenty years, they continued to win IIHF World and Olympic tournaments.

The Canada Cup was developed to recreate the excitement of the 1972 Summit Series. It was a tournament of the best players in the world playing for their own countries. Teams included NHL players. Canada Cup series took place in 1976, 1981, 1984, 1987, and 1991. It later became the World Cup of Hockey and is still played every four years.

In 1975 NHL teams began to draft Soviet players. They hoped one day they could play in the North American league. Nobody knew whether they would ever be able to play in the NHL. At that time, to play in the NHL they had to defect. Defecting meant that they had to leave their country illegally. Most of these players were also officers in the army. Only the Russian government could give them permission to leave legally. And they didn't want to lose their best players.

In 1989 the first Soviet player, Sergei

Priakin, signed an NHL contract. This started the first wave of Soviet players joining the NHL. At first, they were mostly older players let go by Soviet hockey officials. But once Communism in Russia ended, more and more players left freely to play in the NHL. By the 1995–96 season, 55 Russians played for NHL teams.

The Detroit Red Wings won the Stanley Cup in 1997. Three Russians were in their lineup. They brought the Stanley Cup to Russia for the first time. They showed it to fans at the former Communist headquarters in the Red Square in Moscow.

The Soviet Union won their last Olympic gold medal in 1988. By 1991 the Communist-controlled Soviet Union had ended. Leader Mikhail Gorbachev reformed the government. He took steps toward a more democratic system. At the

1992 Olympics, a team made up of the former Soviet Union countries won gold.

The last Canadian team to win a world championship title was the 1961 Trail Smoke Eaters. In 1994 a team of NHLers reclaimed the title after 32 long years.

That same year, without NHL players, Team Canada came within a shootout of winning Olympic gold. But the Olympic gold medal drought would last 50 years for Canada. The 1952 gold medal was the last gold until 2002. That year, an Olympic team of Canadian NHLers won the championship. They struck gold again at the 2010 Olympics in Vancouver.

As the years passed, nobody forgot the 1972 Summit Series. The series became eight of the most important games in hockey history. Victory brought a nation together, cheering as one.

Glossary

Assist: The pass which leads to a goal being scored.

Backhand: A pass or shot that is taken from the backside of the hockey stick blade.

Beat the defence: To get by one or both defencemen.

Blind pass: To pass the puck without looking.

Bodychecking: When a hockey player bumps or slams into an opponent with his body.

Deke or deking: To make a defensive player think you are going to pass or move a certain direction when you are not.

Forwards: The three players who make up the offence or forward line of a team—the centre and right and left wing.

Full-strength: When both teams have all five players and their goalie on the ice.

Intermission: A 15 minute recess between each of the three periods of a hockey game.

One-timer: When a player passes the puck to a teammate who then shoots the puck immediately without stopping the puck first.

Open ice: The part of the ice that is free of opponents.

Passing: When one player uses his stick to send the puck to a teammate.

Penalty: Punishment of a player for breaking the rules.

Rebound: A puck that bounces off the goalie's body or equipment.

Rush: An individual or combined attack by a team carrying the puck.

Save: The act of a goalie blocking or stopping a shot.

Acknowledgements

I was not alive when the 1972 Summit Series took place, so I do not have first-hand experience of the event. Throughout my life I have heard many stories from people who watched it on television. But, instead of using the stories of family and friends to write this book, I used the writings of sports journalists who were at the games.

The books I consulted included *Canada's Olympic Hockey Teams* by Andrew Podnieks, *Team Canada 1972: Where Are They Now?* by Brian McFarlane, *The Greatest Game* by Todd Denault, *The Days Canada Stood Still: Canada vs. USSR 1972* by Scott Morrison, *Cold War: The Amazing Canada-Soviet Hockey Series of 1972* by Roy MacSkimming, *Tretiak:*

The Legend by Vladislav Tretiak, *The Road to Olympus* by Anatoli Tarasov, *War on Ice: Canada in International Hockey* by Scott Young, *Hockey is Our Game* by Jim Coleman, and *Hockey Night in Moscow* by Jack Ludwig. To gain more knowledge about the Soviet Union I read *Canada and the Cold War* by Reg Whitaker and Steve Hewitt.

I watched the complete Summit Series on DVD. This box set was called *'72 Complete: The Ultimate Collector's Edition of the 1972 Summit Series*. I found two documentaries helpful with my research — *'72: From Training Camp to Victory, The Untold Story* and *Summit On Ice: The Shot That Was Heard Around the World*.

I would like to thank my editors Rebecca Sjonger and Carrie Gleason in helping me write this book. I would also like to thank my parents and wife Shelley for their continued support.

About the Author

Richard Brignall is a journalist from Kenora, Ontario. He is a graduate of the University of Manitoba and former managing editor of its student newspaper, *The Manitoban*. He has written articles for *Cottage Life* and *Outdoor Canada*. He was previously a sports reporter for the *Kenora Daily Miner and News*. He is the author of several books in the Recordbooks series. Visit him online at www.richardbrignall.com.

Photo Credits

We gratefully acknowledge the following sources for permission to reproduce the images within this book:

Richard Brignall: cover, 11, 13, 18, 29, 35, 39, 42, 53, 59, 68, 74, 90, 103, 108, 115, 121, 125, 136

Index